TIME FOR KIDS READERS

ELLIS ISLAND

by Susan Ring

Harcourt

Orlando Austin Chicago New York Toronto London San Diego

Visit *The Learning Site!*
www.harcourtschool.com

Long ago, people came to America on big ships. They wanted a better life.

In 1907, a ship filled with many people went to one place first. That place was Ellis Island.

Inside, there was a lot of noise. There were many people from many different places. People waited in the big hall. They took many different kinds of tests. They had to be healthy to stay.

After their long trips, people were hungry. They drank milk. They ate fish and bread with butter.

Some people were at Ellis Island for many days. Some were there for a few days.

The people below are about to leave Ellis Island for their new homes in America.

Today, Ellis Island is a museum. It tells us about the people who came to America long ago.